There's Nowt So Queer As Folk

S. Patricia Clayford

(with Illustrations by the Author)

S. Patricia Clayford

CONTENTS

DEDICATION

To my friend CATH,
who encouraged, cajoled and bullied me, sadly she passed away suddenly before she could see my work in print.

To CONNIE,
who encouraged all she could, praised my work when I had doubts, popped magazines through my letter box every week or so with publishers' advertisements ringed or starred.

To EVERYONE,
who gave me encouragement and the confidence to go ahead.

Last but certainly not least, my love and thanks
to ROY,
my Husband, who gave his time to turn all my longhand scribblings into beautifully neat print and helped me all along the way.

About Myself

Proud of being born and brought up in Yorkshire, I was taken to the tiny hamlet of Wike when only nine months old, where I lived happily until the age of twenty one. Wike then only twenty houses, was a part of Lord Harewood's estate and I attended Harewood village school until I was 14.

A great lover of the countryside, especially the Yorkshire Dales, one of my favourite views is still, descending Harewood Bank from the village to a point where I can see Wharfedale spread out in front of me with Almscliffe Crag dominating the horizon.

I enjoy painting, both in oils and watercolours but never feel I can do the scenery Justice, the colours are so magnificent.

I met Roy, who was in the R A F at the time, when I was almost 17 and we married in Harewood Church when I was 20.

I trained as a Ladies Hairdresser after leaving school but gave it up when our family came along to look after them and to help look after my elderly Mother who had heart trouble.

We have two married children, our Son and his Wife have a business in Cornwall and our Daughter and our three lovely Granddaughters are now back living in Yorkshire after spending twenty years in Zimbabwe.

MILLENIUM FEVER

Couldn't believe what a poor show Leeds put on,
compared with other towns and cities.

Well now it's all ovver after all that theer 'ype,
we've been countin' down t'days for t'past year,
Millenium fever 'ad got us,
there'd be a grand party, no fear.

MILLIONS wa' spent down i' London,
on t'Dome an' them fireworks bi t'ton,
then would it be ready i' time for that neet,
Ee, t'tension wa' buildin', by gum.

We'd Millenium this an' Millenium that
all t'year, it got wors' week bi week,,
then suddenly Christmas wa' ovver
an' t'excitement wa' up to its peak.

twelve o'clock cem an' we watched on TV,
from city to city we went,
fireworks exploded an' t'parties went on,
it wa' worth every penny they'd spent.

Us Loiners, we then watched i' wonder,
to see what OUR city 'ad planned,
'Ow could we contain all t'excitement,
mebbe — Fireworks an' Dancin', — a Band?

To Chapeltown then we went ovver,
an' we saw this uncarpeted place,
wi' a bloke carryin' up - sound equipment,
of owt else ther' just wasn't a trace.

Back off round t'country we travelled,
Reporter's wa' workin' like 'eck,
to bring us t'momentous occasion,
even Philip an' t'Queen 'ad a peck.

1

The' even 'eld 'ands an' sang 'Auld Lang Syne',
wi' Tony, Cherie, Folks galore,
in t'Dome the' wa' SO much excitement,
an occasion like nivver before.

An' THEN back to LEEDS the' returned us,
amid this excitement — on cue —
an theer sat a bloke an' a kid on a wall,
wi' a SPARKLER!! LEEDS wa' that t'best you could do?

THE FRENCH WOMAN

A funny incident on a couples trip to France.

A couple of bikers I 'eard of
decided to go on a tour.
France wa' to be t'destination
so off went that bike wi' a roar.

The' crossed over t'sea on a ferry,
a reight big adventure for sure,
the' rode on for miles after t'crossing
an' rode 'til the' couldn't ride no more.

The' wa' tired, the' wa' stiff, the' wa' 'ungry,
so the' stopped when the' got out o' t'town,
put a match to the'r stove an' med sarnies
stretched the'r legs, then on t'grass, the' sat down.

Now just over t'road, stood this woman,
who watched 'em —- an' paced up an' down,
the' wondered if p'raps she wa' thirsty
an' she wa' t'only person around.

'E put down 'is tea 'an poured 'er some,
cos after all, t'tea it wa' med.
So 'E crossed over t'road to this woman,
she seemed grateful an' "Merci" she said.

He said, "Do you think that she's 'ungry"?
'is Wife said "She could be – I s'pose",
'cos she wa' still standin' theer lookin'
"I'll give 'er some food —- 'fore she goes.

'E picked up a sandwich an' over 'e went,
"Merci" she said gladly, once more
but when she 'ad 'et it, she still stood around
an' the' wanted to get off on t'tour.

Puzzled, the' looked an' the' wondered,
she'd e'tten an' drank —- wi' no fuss,
then all of a sudden, she smiled an' she waved
as she clambered up t'steps of a BUS!!

AN' 'ERE IS THE NEWS

This poem is just a sign of the times and was written
when I'd become really fed up with all the bad news.

I don't think we're meant to be 'appy
it don't seem much like it to me,
if YOU wekken up feelin' cheerfull
it won't LAST......I'll guarantee.

The MEDIA, as the' like to call it,
a'll bombard yer wi' all t'doom an' gloom.
Papers an' TV a'll get yer
Before yer even gerrout o' t'room.

A gunman 'as got somebody 'ostage
an' t'streets full o' them armed police,
a megaphone amplifies t'voice o' that cop,
askin' if 'eel please release........

The woman an' child that wer' tekken....
an' will yer please throw out yer gun,
the frozen Reporter stands theer wi' 'er mike
she's been theer since it all begun.

She's doin' 'er best but it's freezin',
she's wishin' that bloke ad come out,
then suddenly,.....it's back to the studio,
they've MORE strife to tell yer about.

A bank robber 'eld somebody at knifepoint
an' gorraway wi' a very large sum.
The Police want to question a fella',
that the' know to be out on the run.

Don't approach 'im they say 'cos 'ees dangerous.
I reckon I've got no INTENTION.
Then the' tell yer to not let yer kids go to school,
it's burnt down ....'cos a lad got DETENTION!!

Me cornflakes are beginnin' to stick in me throat,
me tea's goin' cold in me cup,
a'm that bloomin' MAD, wi' all that's goin' on,
it reight meks yer want to give up.

I think to meself, a'l read t'paper
as I 'ead out to t'shops on a bus
but is ther' owt cheerful to brighten you up?
you've got to be jokin' - becos......

'eadlines the' yell out ther's more sorror,
another poor soul wi' 'Mad Cow',
ther's 'UNDREDS a cows to be slaughtered
so t'Farmers are then wond'rin' 'ow....

the'll manage to cope 'til it's sorted
an' will EUROPE one DAY lift that ban,
will OWT ever get back to normal,
like before all this trouble began?

Ther's a suicide agen, in a prison,
a sex offender's out on the loose,
a VERY old woman is tied up and robbed,
by a bloke full o' cocaine an' booze.

What do yer think says a neighbour,
our Post Office up t'street 'as been done
an' t'missis next door 'as been burgled,
when the'd gone on a break for some sun,

they've ransacked the place, med a REIGHT mess,
you'd never believe, 'less yer see.
Oh! for Pete's sake a'm gerrin' a 'eadache,
can't wait to ger 'ome for some tea.

Oh! t'suns come out now..... that feels better
but what's on that board goin' by?
I REALLY don't want to believe what it says,
THE KINGDOM OF 'EAVEN IS NIGH.

FREDDIES FLIGHT

Believe it or not I read in the paper
about a woman who sent her Husbands
ashes up on a rocket, at his request. It
just appealed to my silly sense of humour.

Theer goes our Fred, did ta see 'im?
'es gone whizzin' by on that stick,
the' said it wa' just what 'e wanted,
it seems a reight queer way to pick.

Could 'ave 'ad a posh urn, sat on t'sideboard,
same as most other folk do
but NO, 'e 'ad a yen to go flyin',
so she did as 'e wished, did our Sue.

She gor 'er sen stocked up wi' rockets,
got permission to fire 'em in t'sky'
'ad 'em all specially adapted,
then Freddie wa' all set to fly.

Neighbours looked out i' amazement,
wind dropped an' our Fred cem to land,
strange powder wa' coverin' t'gardens,
the' thowt it must be t'desert sand.

Anyway, time went by an' would you believe,
our Sue, who'd been thinkin' ahead,
went out an' she bowt some more rockets,
'cos she'd kept back a bit of our Fred.

WELL t'Millenium cem, an' 'is
dream it cem true,
imagine that smile on 'is face,
wi' a scream an' a bang, 'e went
shootin' off,
now 'e's floatin about, out i'
space.

6

ASHES TO ASHES

This poem I wrote after going to a funeral,
only to discover that the deceased wasn't our
relation at all. It is all absolutely true,
even the swinging chandeliers.

'Ave you ever gatecrashed a funeral?
Well it 'appened to us t'other day,
we turned up at t'church all respectful,
to 'elp poor owd lad on 'is way.

We'd read all about it int' paper,
it did seem alreight at the time,
wit' reight name an' age, even t'district,
it must be t'alf Brother o' thine.

We'd 'eard that 'ed moved from the district
an' some'ow we seemed to lose touch,
then when we read of 'is passin',
we thowt, well, we could go to t'chuch.

Well t'funeral wa' reight ovver i' Filey,
next day we wer' off afore leet,
sixty odd miles we'd to travel,
an' then we got summat to eat.

Now t'chuch wa' reight opposite t'caffy,
an' we sheepishly went reight up to it,
when all of a sudden, a chap oppened t'door,
sayin', "Come in, it will start in a minute".

We wa' tecken aback, but we did as 'e said,
an' sat us sens down int' back pew,
tryin' to mek out t'congregation,
was ther anyone theer that we knew?

The Fisherman's choir, they sang i' one voice,
a sound that wa' movin' an' deep,
then t'Son talked about 'is late Father,
so touchin', it fair med yer weep.

7

E'd been a grand chap an' thowt well on,
judgin' bi that congregation,
we kept sneakin' a look at t'other folk theer,
could 'e 'ave been our relation?

Ther's one that ah think looks a bit like yer Dad,
an seems to 'ave same coloured 'air
could 'e be a cousin ah wonder,
if only we knew who wa' there.

An' as we sat theer contemplatin'
I appened to glance up at leet,
an' would yer believe — it wa' movin,
as sure as am 'ere it wa' — reight,

Ah looked up at leet, an' ah looked towards t'door,
an ah thowt well ther must be a draught,
but leet, it wer 'evvy, an t'door, it wa' shut,
oh crikey! ah must be goin' daft.

Ah kept sneakin' a look at that chandelier thing,
as faster an' faster it swung,
an all of a sudden ah wanted to laugh
as last movin' 'ymn, it wa' sung.

It wa' mebbe a message to tell us
that WE shouldn't be theer that day,
gatecrashin' a funeral is not reight at all,
whatever would anyone say?

Well t'Preacher 'E went an' 'E stood up by t'door
sheckin' 'ands as we all med to leave,
'e told us that we should go for some tea,
"Everyone's asked, I believe".

Well we waited 'til t'last, so that we could explain,
an' tell 'im that p'raps we shouldn't stay,
but 'e said to go an' meet t'famly,
"Now that you've come all this way".

8

Well,we climbed up them stairs an we went into t'room,
full of friends an' relations — all talkin',
bi then I wa' wishin' we'd gone through t'chuch door,
as fast as we could — an' kept walkin'.

Well t'Son spotted us an' cem ovver,
'e did seem a very nice lad,
we explained that 'e might be related
"'E might be t'alf brother o' yer Dad."

Now t'lad looked a wee bit astonished
shook 'ands an' 'e wanted to 'ear,
about this strange branch o' the famly
that 'ad come all that way to be theer.

Ah sez, "Does yer Dad 'ave a Brother,
older than 'im. an called Les",
he sez, "No, my uncle's called Thomas,
so, it can't be the same one, I guess".

More we asked questions an' more we could tell
we wer barkin up wrong tree for sure
but 'e asked us to stop an 'ave "somethin' to eat"
but we wanted to get through that door

'E insisted that we 'ad a cuppa,
so we drank it an' said we wa' sorry,
'e said, "It is good that you've come all this way".
So we thanked 'im, an' left in a 'urry.

When we got outside, we could do nowt but laugh,
cos it did seem a strange thing to be, ,
gatecrashin' a funeral i' Filey,
It could only 'appen to me ....

IS THERE ANYBODY THERE?

*This happened to two ladies we knew who were
very anxious to have their fortunes told.*

Ther' once wa' a woman, or so I 'eard tell,
decided to visit a 'Teller',
she wanted to contact t'departed
an' this woman wa' good, said this fella'.

She drove off one night wi' 'er daughter
couldn't wait to 'ear WHAT she'd foretell,
an' WHO she would manage to contact,
so they dashed up to t'ouse an' rung t'bell.

Well, the' waited an' waited an' nobody cem'
so the' knocked 'ard as well, to mek sure.
The' thowt she might BE wi' a client,
'cos STILL nobody answered that door.

The' waited a bit, then decided to try
to oppen it a bit an' then shout,
so the' gev it a shove an in the' both went
an' ther' wa'n't anybody about.

Off t'passage wa this room which the' entered
an' just one old man who sat theer,
so she whispered "Ther's just one afore us"
an' said "Oh it's quite nice in 'ere".

A table wa' stood theer in t'middle,
wi' one or two books spread about,
the' read t'magazines while the' waited,
an' t'clairvoyant she never cem out.

The' said to t'old man, "Are YOU waitin'
or 'ave you been in an' been seen?
she's tekkin' a long time wi' someb'dy".
'E says, "Ah don't know what you mean".

'E says, "Who are you, I don't know ya',
an' WHO 'ave you been waitin' for?".
The' said "Well we've come to see t'psychic".
'E says, "Well tha should be next door"!!!.

10

NOT PINK ELEPHANTS
BLACK DOGS!!

A visit to my Brother-in-law and his dog Oscar.

We'd been out an' gor all us presents
an' this year we'd bowt 'im some socks,
cos 'is dowter said that's what 'e wanted,
so it sorted one more christmas box.

To 'is 'ouse we went off to deliver
our present all carefully wrapped
an' as we gor on to 'is backyard,
we wer' all just a little bit capped,

'cos OUTSIDE 'is gate theer sat Oscar,
we 'oped that ther' wa'nt summat up.
'E wa' nivver allowed out o' t'gate theer,
since 'e'd wandered, when 'e wa' a pup.

We med a big fuss an' we told 'im,
that 'e wa' a reight naughty lad,
but shocked a bit, 'ow 'e wa' lookin',
thowt 'e'd aged an' 'e looked a bit bad.

It wa'n't THAT long since I'd seen 'im,
but 'is coat didn't look quite so bright,
tho' 'is tail it wa' waggin', 'e med a reight fuss
so I thowt p'raps e's REALLY alright.

We unbolted t'gate an' we took 'im inside,
sayin' "Oscar, lets go see yer Dad",
we knocked 'ard on t'door an' we shouted
then we thowt that we must be going mad,

'cos straight out o' t'house bounded Oscar
wi' a coat that wa' all bright an' shiny,
leapin' an' lickin', all excited,
full o' life an' not quite as tiny......

As t'other black dog, — that 'ad moved in next door,
who could 'ave been our Oscar's twin,
but it turned out that she wa' a lady
an' Oscar a definite 'IM........

11

CHRISTMAS IS COMING

"It's nearly Christmas" she announced one day,
it cem reight out o' t'blue
"We'd better start gerrin t'presents
or I'll have too much ter do".

'E peeped ovver top o' t'paper
t'news filled 'im wi' alarm,
'e thowt, oh! 'ere we go again
but I'll try an' keep me calm,

"Well don't go buyin' t'shops up,
we wont DO so much this year
we've got to pull us 'orns in".
'E wa'n't feeling much good cheer.

'E ducked back behind 'is paper
an' saw that Leeds 'ad won
but t'joy wa'n't theer no longer
wit' shoppin' to be done

'E tried again, a different tack,
"Do THEY all buy for you?
three 'undred pounds ah spent last year
THAT we just can't do"!

She reminded 'im of Freddy
an' Alice an' 'er Mother
you can't spend £10 on one of 'em
wi'out doin' same for t'other

Ther's yer sisters, mine as well,
yer Brothers Ted an' Jim
an' then ther' wives, as well as t'kids,
an t'next door, ther's Er an' Im.

'E wa' loosin' ground an' no mistake
it wa' gerrin worse bi't' minnit,
but she said "ah'll try an' do me best
to keep wi'in are limit".

Off she went wi' bulgin purse,
an' shopped an' shopped all day,
opin' 'e wouldn' go rantin,
wi' spendin' all 'is pay.

She staggered 'ome wi' t'parcels,
struggled wi' 'em onto t'bus
she saw 'is face 'an said reight sharp,
"Thers one or two for us"

When t'christmas mornin' cem around
an they sat in't debris theer,
torn up paper, bits o' string
but she NEARLY shed a tear.

A little pile stood on one side,
an' what do you think wa' theer,
a box o' talc, an 'anky,
an' a can o' strongish beer,

a tie i' garish colours,
an' a pair o' yeller socks,
sum mintoes an' a bar o' soap
done up in a fancy box.

She says "Ah think yer reight, yer know
but its supposed to be the THOUGHT
ther' i'nt much stuff to show for
ALL that stuff WE bought".

"Next year we'll 'ave a re-think
an' I'll listen to what yer say
in t'meantime, drink yer beer up
HAPPY CHRISTMAS DAY"!......

MERRY
XMAS

13

OUT ON THE TOWN
SAT'DAY NEET I' WAKEFIELD

*This Yorkshire poem was written after we had been
to Wakefield for a meal one winters night.*

Ther's summat that I can't quite fathom,
'Ave thowt about it quite a lot,
why t'young 'uns go out i' midwinter,
dressed like the' think that it's 'OT,

When WE go to Wakefield at nighttime,
when t'brass monkey's are quakin' wi fear
an' WE'RE muffled up to us eyebrows,
as t'first flakes o' snow they appear.

Ther's t'young 'uns out theer, off t'disco's
to t'bars an to t'night clubs i' droves,
but as the' go by, a'h just WONDER,
A' think they've forgotten ther' cloze.

Wheer ar' ther' coats an' ther' jackets?
what bekem o' ther' boots, scarves an' mitts,
good grief, just look ovver at that one,
the'r in for a shock, when she sits.

Ther's one theer, in't little black number,
it's sleeveless an' backless an' thin,
'Er legs seem to go forever,
ah swear the' go up to 'er chin.

T'lads ar' out 'untin' a' reckon,
ther' off out ont' town for the night,
just in ther' trouziz an' shirtsleeves,
ther' int even a 'pully' i' sight.

Well I want to know wot is 'appenin',
why I can't keep warm — wish a' could
ah think it must be t'lukewarm watter,
that runs through me veins — stead o' blood.

LONG IN THE TOOTH

This one speaks for itself.

Now that we each have a bus pass,
a' reckon we've got to admit,
that we ARE a pair of old stagers,
and ARE gerrin on just a bit.

There's bottles o' pills on the table
all lined up an' ready to tek,
ther's specs an' spec cases all lyin' around
to see wi', if we keep awek.

Our TV's on, ovver in't corner,
I'm readin the paper as well,
e's slumped in 'is chair, fast asleep, so it seems,
but, e's restin' 'is eyes for a spell.

Every day we find out somethin' different
that WE never thowt of before,
why some old folks 'omes are so dusty,
wi' bits an' breadcrumbs on the floor.

My 'ouse, a' thowt it wa' spotless
as me polish went on wi' a squirt,
but ONE day ah' put on mi glasses
an the damned place wa' covered i' dirt.

It lurked round the knobs on the cooker,
it 'id in each crevice an' crack.
T'edges o't tiles wa'n't white anymore,
but 'eadin' from grey into black.

THEN a' think that a'll just do some sewin',
it won't tek much more than a minute
an' ten minutes later a'm still pokin' t'thread
at that needle, an' WILL it go in it?

15

The thread is wet through from goin' into mi mouth,
to smooth it an' mek it reight thin,
but as soon as it touches me needle,
it fans out an' it WILL not go in.

SOMETIMES, I'm patient an' do it at last,
an sometimes I'm NOT in the mood
an' say what a' think about this gettin' owd,
an' sometimes it's even quite rude.

A' used to see women wi' lipstick,
That looked like the'd been in the jam
ther rouge wa' i' little red patches
wi' powder i' splotches o' tan.

But now that I'M gettin' me pension,
at last it's come all clear to me,
of COURSE the' can't put on the'r make-up,
wi' no specs, the poor beggars can't see.

So just you remember you young 'uns,
when laughin' at strange things we do,
I wa' laughin' mesen, not that long since,
an ONE day, it'll 'appen to YOU.

THE PERILS OF THE BUS PASS

I was quite looking forward to being Sixty and
thinking of the advantages of having a bus-pass,
but sometimes things are not as rosy as they appear.

Me friend said " You'll soon 'ave yer bus pass,
we'll be able to travel all ovver,
just go to t'post office wi' t'photo,
yer pay, an' it i'nt any bother"

So as soon as it got past me birthday,
off to t'post office a' sped,
an' t'chap couldn't BELIEVE a' wa' SIXTY,
"A'd NEVER a thowt it", 'e said.

A wa' tellin' a friend all about it,
when sharin' a nice pot o' tea,
me ego wa' quickly deflated,
when she said,"Oh 'e said that to me",

But then a' wa' DYIN' to use it
this grand little card that a'd bowt,
just to 'op on a bus an' pay tenpence,
the WORLD is me OYSTER a' thowt.

DISCREETLY a' flashed it at t'driver,
not wantin' all t'bus load to see
that a' now wa' an O.A.P. proper,
driver GLARED an 'e then YELLED at me,

"THAT'S no good before it's NINE THIRTY"
an' ALL t'other passenger's could 'ear,
"You'll 'ave to pay 'alf price at THIS time,
it's THIRTY FIVE PENCE — do yer 'ear?"

Bi' then mi face looked like a beetroot,
it WA'NT workin' out like a' thowt,
so I tried to sit down — a bit fast like,
not before 'e shot off wi' a jolt.

A poor bloke 'e looked very startled,
as a' med a quick grab at a seat,
a' said that a' wa' very SORRY,
I'd TRIED not to land on 'is feet.

We jerked an we swerved all the way theer,
a toddler it screamed, — a man swore,
a woman 'ad a set to wi' t'driver,
said she wished that she'd caught bus before.

Then somebody cem runnin' to t'bus stop
all red faced an' clutchin"er fare
but 'e shut 'is doors in a hurry
an drove off — as IF she wa'nt there.

At last a' reached MY destination
an' 'e whizzed round t'corner reight fast,
'e looked t'other way an' ignored me,
as I told 'im that we'd gone reight past,

"A' thowt t'stop wa' theer, just round t'corner",
a' said, — but 'e din't want to 'ear,
'e put 'is foot down an' kept goin'
an' pretended that I wasn't theer.

A'd to walk all t'way back an' wa' fumin',
met me friend an' told 'er what 'e'd done,
she'd seen 'im an come up to meet me,
a' said it i'nt REALLY much fun,

We all 'ave us bad days, o' some kind,
at least 'es a job — drivin' t'bus
can't the' just smile an' be pleasant,
ONE day , THEY'LL be oldies like US.

THE WHITBY T(D)RIP
or we WILL enjoy it!

A true story of our day-trip to Whitby
and was written on our way home.

Our Pensioners club 'ad a meeting,
to plan all us Trips out for t'year.
The' studied things ovver an' then the' announced,
the'd come up wi' loads of ideas!!

Well on t'first one we'd all go to Whitby
but Pickering 'ud be us first call,
where we'd get on an old fashioned 'chuffer'
it'd chug ovver t'moors wi' us all.

At last the day cem' — 12th of April,
an' t'weather forecast wa'nt so good,
we got on t'coach theer at AGFA,
it wa' rainin', but the' warned us it would.

Well it di'n't get much better as t'miles we e't up,
then at Pickerin' we all got off t'bus .
first 'eadin' for t'toilets an' t'café,
that WEATHER wouldn't spoil it for US.

Train wa' reight comfy an' t'scenery great
but sky wa' all leaden an' grey,
yet as we chugged by all that beauty
we said, "No, it WON'T spoil our day".

We got back on t'bus after t'train ride,
then to Whitby for just after one,
rain it wa' just a bit 'eavier
but we WON'T let it go spoil us fun.

We then 'eaded straight for a café,
we'd been there before — now an' then
but what did we see when we got theer,
just a ruin, a crane an' some men!!.

T'place 'ad been gutted — one Sund'y,
burnt out, we wa' told by some folk,
but we WON'T let it go spoil our day theer
an' we'll mek t'weather a bit of a joke.

Up went t'umb'rella as t'day it got 'worse'
an' we TRIED to find somewhere to eat,
searchin' for somewhere we fancied,
goin' up an' down all o' them streets..

We cut through a 'ginnel' — still lookin',
mi' brolly wa' firmly in place,
'til a big gust o' wind left me 'olding it's shaft
an' t'rest of it COVERED Roy's face.

But we WON'T let it spoil our outin',
as we ditched them two bits in a bin.
Then we cem' to a nice FISH & CHIP shop
an' as t'rain it lashed down —- we went in.

We 'ad a nice meal — an' got drier,
sat theer 'til we thowt we'd best go,
couldn't stop in t'café forever
though it wa' very temptin' —- an' so —-

Now minus mi' brolly an' mi' beret in place,
we walked through all t'rain to this shop,
which advertised t'Whitby museum,
so we climbed up all t'steps —- reight to t'top.

A' sez it's no wonder that they only charge
a quid to show t'pensioners ther' wares,
a' reckon it's nowt short of a miracle
that WE even med' it upstairs.

Well it killed 'alf an hour out o' that rain
an' Woolworth's wa' t'next port o' call
we thowt we could just 'ave a wander
but ther' wa' nowt much to see theer at all.

Four o'clock cem' an we went for some tea
an we sat theer as long as we could,
the' ended up puttin' up t'shutters
the' said we could stop —- the' were good.

At last it wa' time, we could go get on t'bus,
all wet an' bedraggled — —an'TRIED —-
to say that damned weather just didn't spoil our day
but we'd 'ave to admit that WE LIED.

20

INTO AFRICA

*A few years ago we flew to Zimbabwe to see our
only Daughter and her lovely family who lived there.
This poem tells the story of our journey.*

Our Daughter said "Come to Zimbabwe"—
so we thowt that we WOULD do us best
to save up an' go see all t'famly,
as two years 'ad gone by since last.....

we'd seen all our lovely Grandchildren,
we knew the'd 'ave altered a bit,
so we saved an we planned for a visit,
then booked t'plane an' t'coach for our trip.

We travelled to London from Moortown,
just called in, to pick up, in Leeds.
Then t'coach carried on wi'out stoppin',
the' catered for all of us needs.

No stoppin' for 'loos' or a sandwich,
they 'ad all that we needed on board,
wi' a courier who spoke reight broad Yorkshire
an chatted wi' t'driver all t'road.

When WE got to London Victoria,
the' dropped out us cases from t'old,
we crossed ovver t'road wi t'wheels rattlin',
and went to find t'place we wa' told.

We sat theer t'best part of an 'our
an' et' rest of us snap wi' some tea,
fed t'pigeons an' birds that wa' in theer,
them seats wa' as COLD as could be.

We wa' reight glad to see t'bus to Gatwick,
we wa' t'first theer in t'queue — — — 'im an' me,
"Do you want Norf or Sarf?" says the driver,
we din't know — - an' neither did 'e.

In an hour or so we reached t'airport
an we cem to t'south part, at long last,
sez t'driver "I'd ger orf at this wan,
you can SOON ger acrors, if ya mast."

We staggered from t'bus wi us cases
an true to 'Sods Law' — —- yes it's true,
of course it wa' t'NORTH SIDE we wanted,
so we went to find out, what to do.

Now t'train wa' a wee bit elusive,
'cos we got out o' t'lift, just to find,
a dirty gret big escalator
an' a slope like a mountain, round t'side,

we thowt that we must be mistaken,
so went back in t'lift, tried agen,
but finished up BACK wheer we STARTED,
me spirits wa' sinkin' an' then..........

A young man an' girl saw us standin',
realizin' our plight, grabbed a case,
an strode off an up t'escalator,
so we then did us best to keep pace.

We thanked 'im an' sed we wa' grateful,
it WA' such a kind thing for sure,
as our cases the' wa' very 'eavy
an' we 'ad to get up to t'next floor.

At last we could then get a trolley
an' went for this train, a STRANGE thing,
it wa' like a LIFT door that we went through,
us an' trolley then went OFF — — wi' a ring.

As smooth as could be wa' this journey,
in no time we got to t'north side
an' able to part wi' us cases
but our booked seats were gone, — — well we tried.

Travel Agent 'ad said we could book 'em,
so we did it all ovver our phone,
we'd picked two nice seats bi a 'winder,'
fixed it afore we left 'ome ....Well,

we 'ad some more tea while we waited,
an' went an' looked round t'duty free,
then before very long we wa' boardin',
an'' TOOK OFF'' at just seven twenty three

The Steward waved 'is arms, like the' 'ave to,
Oxygen masks an' life jackets to see
but nobody teks any notice,
the'r waitin to buy t'duty free.

T'trolley cem round an' then t'dinner,
Lamb 'Ot Pot, wi starters an' sweet,
a veritable FEAST we wa' given,
wi' t'free wine — —- cheese an' biscuits to eat.

The' put on a film to amuse us,
which WE felt too tired to see,
so we thowt that we WOULD try an' settle
an' for once get some sleep ..... 'opefully

Folks 'ad changed all ther seats an' wa' sprawlin'
so 'e went a few rows up t'plane,
so that 'e could put 'is feet up
an' thowt a' could mebbe do t'same

.

The' give yer a blanket an' pillow,
to mek sure yer warm durin' t'night,
but YOU try an' get yersen comfy,
a CONTORTIONIST might be alright.

Yer put t'pillow on t'winder, yer necks in a crick,
shuffle down, yer legs stick out in t'aisle
to trip all t'folks up when ther' off down to t'loo,
or ther' stretchin' ther' legs for a while.

Everyone's shufflin' an tryin' to sleep,
BALLOONS are now what once wer' feet,
yer nose is dried out an' yer limbs are so stiff,
yer doubt if yer CAN move from t'seat.

Hour after hour, this torture goes on
an' at last ther's a light theer in t'sky,
apart from all t'lightnin' that's flashed all through t'night.
Dawn 'as broken, so now t'end is nigh.

We all 'ad a very nice breakfast,
then t'folk wa' all queuein' in t'aisle
clutchin' sponge bags an' standin' theer cross legged,
as the' knew the'd be waitin' a while.

At last it wa' "Fasten yer seatbelts",
we're mekkin' a start to descend,
then suddenly, flaps down an' some music,
we really ARE gettin' to t'end.

Through t'winder we saw t'airport buildin'
an folk viewin' from t'veranda, up theer
 we THEN said goodbye to our Steward,
cem down t'steps wi' a sigh an' a prayer.

Then we wa' crossin' the tarmac,
ther's little blonde 'eads theer a' SWEAR,
an THEN, all the rest o' the famly
were WAVIN' to welcome us there.

The journey it soon wa' forgotten,
as we 'ugged an' we kissed everyone,
it's good to be back i' Zimbabwe.......
THIS time, just 'ope we get SUN.

RAIN - DANCE

Places we've been in the rain!

Thinkin' one day about t'olidays,
are other folk ever the same?
everywhere we seem to go to
it decides that it might as well rain.

EVEN before we were married,
to Scarboro we thowt we would go
an' we'd get engaged on Roy's birthday,
THAT day it decided to SNOW!!!

In t'70's we went down to Cornwall,
wi' a case full o' nice summer togs,
but what did it do when we got theer?
it rained an' it rained CATS AN' DOGS.

NEW to us this caravannin',
for Michael, 'is mate, Roy an' me,
we thowt it'd be reight relaxin'.
Ther'd be sunshine an' sand an' blue sea!!.

Leisurely strolls round the village,
mebbe trips out to sea on the boats
but theer we wer muffled to't' eyebrows,
in polo necked sweaters an' coats.

Caravan wa' a luxury model,
t'length a fair number o' feet
it wa' spacious - an streamlined - a beauty
but what we missed most wa' some HEAT!!

Now by t'80's we really wa' mobile,
wi' a motor'ome parked up outside.
Now t'world wa' our oyster, we reckoned,
off into t'sunset we'd ride

But some'ow things don't seem to 'appen
not QUITE like yer planned in yer dreams.
Work seems to tek all yer time up,
also people —- an' things —- so it seems.

But we DID plan a fortnight i' Scotland,
30 years I'd been promised that tour,
but when Friday night cem an' we'd to pack t'van
that rain it just did now't but pour.

On't Sat'dy we couldn't load t'van up
as it cem down i' torrents all day
ever 'opeful we watched every forecast
reight fed up wi' that long delay.

Next day it took us 'til teatime,
to ger all us gear packed away,
up an' down t'path between t'showers
determined to get off THAT day.

Forecast wa'nt reight good for Scotland,
tho' int' WEST it might JUST be alright.
We spent us first night close to Gretna,
rain rattled on t'roof all through t'night.

T'scenery we thowt it wa' lovely,
as we stared between t'wipers an' t'drops
'ow WONDERFUL if it wa' sunny,
it'll look really GRAND when it stops.

Up t'west coast we drove — ever 'opeful,
t'forecast we used as a guide,
mebbe ovver int' east 'ud be better
we thowt — as we crossed to THAT side.

We passed by LOCH NESS —- but no monster,
Caledonian canal —- Inverness,
there t'locals said it 'ad been fine 13 WEEKS,
could 'ardly believe it but YES ——-

No rain AT ALL, they all told us
an' it REALLY wa' t'wrong time o' t'year.
For Scotland, it's best spring or autumn.
Roy's "hols" they wa' JULY that year.

We saw Aberdeen —-t'granite city
an' no doubt in t'sun it looked grand
but in t'rain it wa' greyer than ever,
wi' one man an' 'is dog on the sand.

We tried East an' West, now in t'Middle,
wa' where we thowt we'd better 'ead,
at least it might not be as windy
an' it COULD just be drier, we said.

We saw t'River Dee an' Balmoral,
even managed a photo or two,
as we trundled along in our motor,
int' rain that wa' best we could do.

One night we parked up in a village,
saw t'STARS as all t'clouds cleared away,
t'HIGHLAND GAMES are goin' on 'ere tomorrer,
if it's nice we might stop 'ere for t'day.

Well no doubt, you've guessed just what 'appened,
bi' mornin' on t'winders t'rain lashed,
we peeped out o' t'curtains — — fair sickened
as into all t'pools t'rain it splashed.

I tried. "Well it MIGHT improve later,
be nice to see t'games while we're 'ere",
Roy said "I'M not wearin' me wellies,
to trail around t'wet fields — — so theer"........

So back HOME we cem a day early,
so much for my 30 year yen,
to see Bonnie Scotland i' summer
an' we've never been back theer agen.

Now PORTUGAL wa' t'next place for raincoats,
Roy retired — — an' t'next thing we knew,
it wa' 'eart attacks, 'ospitals, a by-pass,
all that lot just cem out o' t'blue.

Well as soon as 'e felt a bit better
an' the' gev' 'im the O.K. to go,
We booked us a fortnight in t'sunshine,
then flew off to Faro — — an' so — —

We 'ired a car theer at t'airport.
Our 'oliday — — at last its begun.
It looked grey as we went towards t'Border
we were longin' for blue skies an' sun.

Well t'hotel it wa' lovely, t'place it wa' grand
but bi' t'time we arrived, rain it fell,
went on 10 DAYS out of our fortnight,
a' think we cast some sort o' spell.

To Zimbabwe we've been in their winter,
when t'rain should 'ave stopped weeks before,
but t'rain it 'as come down in torrents,
even much worse than WE'VE seen before.

T'rose garden it sat in a sea o' red mud,
trees 'ave come down , just up t'road
water 'as run like a river,
as down t'footpaths an' t'roads it 'as flowed.

Time before t'last, we wa' theer for 8 weeks
an' you'll 'ardly believe it wa' reight
but, true as i'm sittin' 'ere writin'
it POURED 7 weeks out of 8.

At last, now I've come to t'conclusion .
That if WE play us cards reight —- no joke.
Drought areas might pay us a fortune,
to go theer an' give THEM a SOAK ....

A TRIP TO SHEFFIELD

A day out to try to promote my book—
and of course — it rained!!!

One day Roy an' me went to Sheffield,
wit' aim o' promotin' me book.
cos nobody knows me from Adam,
we thowt the' might just tek a look

As we drove off down't road t'sky got blacker,
it looked like a downpour we feared
an' just as we got near to Sheffield,
on't windscreen t'first rainspots appeared.

We parked up our car and as usual,
t'priority wa' to find t'nearest loo,
then nearby we spotted a cafe,
where we went for a drink, like yer do.

Next job wa' to get t'information,
so at t'centre we dripped through ther' door,
where the' kindly lent us t'yeller pages,
for t'bookshops that we'd to look for.

Roy copied down all o' these bookshops,
then t'lass looked at list wi' a frown,
she says, "I'm right sorry to tell yer
but most of this lot 'ave closed down".

She crossed a lot off an' then told us
about_ t'places THAT we could visit.
Sheffield Scene wa' then t'first place we cem to.
Bedraggled an' wet we went in it.

T'owner she was very 'elpful
an' said SHE would order that day,
even told us just who we should contact
an' she rang a bloke up right away.

She said we should try t'local paper
an' we did as she said —- 'ad a go —-
but 'E wouldn't print owt about me
med' it plain that 'E di'n't want to know

'E said that as WE weren't from Sheffield,
'E couldn't do OWT for me book.
I said "I thowt Yorkshire wa' Yorkshire",
but 'E just wa'n't 'aving no truck.

Be then we wa' soaked an wa' sickened,
we reckoned that we'd 'ad enough.
So we gev 'em a book at the 1st shop,
before staggerin' to t'car, lookin' rough.

At quarter past four we wa' leavin'
an be then t'rain 'ad stopped, weren't we GLAD
ther' wa' even a glimmer o' sunshine,
so drivin' 'ome shouldn't be so bad.

T'motorway wa'n't all that busy,
as on t'M1 we 'eaded for 'ome,
then suddenly t'car started jerkin'
but we struggled up t'ill to reach t'phone.

T'owd car coughed an' spluttered like blazes,
on t'ard shoulder we cem to a stop,
be then a thowt t'thing wa' on fire,
our car it wa' blowin' its top.

Roy got out an' lifted its bonnet,
steam hissed an' shot out wi' such force.
T'engin' wa' red 'ot an' boilin',
bloomin' thing it just seemed to get worse.

T'traffic roared by that 'ard shoulder,
as we waited for 'elp to appear,
an t'wind an all t'noise wa' unnervin',
all t'lorries an' cars seemed that near.

The' tell yer, yer SHOULD climb up t'bankin',
as folks the' get killed standin' theer
but wi' two foot o' nettles an' thistles,
couldn't face it, as my legs were bare.

That cold wind it blew as we stood theer,
so a' chanced it an' sat down in t'car.
We wer' windblown an' shiverin' at t'roadside,
I wa' <u>wishin'</u> we 'adn't gone so far.

Ah got out again an' stood watchin',
for this Breakdown thing to appear,
we'd bin waitin' about twenty minutes
when it zoomed up an' stopped — — nowhere near.

Must a' thowt that 'e wa' a 'Boy-Racer',
as 'e shot on t'ard shoulder that fast,
grit flyin', 'e wa' still doin' seventy
an' stopped about fifty yards past .

'E wa'n't that much slower reversin'
an screeched to a 'alt just in front.
T'door it flew oppen an out jumped this lad,
a reight Yorkshire lad — — was 'e blunt?

'E looked like a beanpole, but 'with it',
baseball cap wrong road round on 'is 'ead,
'e looked under t'bonnet an' tinkered,
we'd 'ave to be towed back, 'e said.

'E said 'e could tow us to Barnsley,
Eighty two pounds to go theer
or for £20 more we could come all t'way 'ome,
we thowt —- No, not Barnsley —- no fear.

Be then t'time wer' goin' an we'd 'ave to get'ome
be train or be bus, well some'ow,
we'd then 'ave to get t'car from Barnsley,
so, "It's best if we tek it 'ome now.

So t'lad 'e then started to fix t'car on t'back,
reight used to t'job, we could see,
talkin' to Roy while 'e did it
an 'e then chanced to look round at me.

'E brok' off an' shoved t'bench seat forrard,
finesse wa' one thing 'e did lack,
as 'e went back 'e shouted t'instructions,
just three little words, "Gerr int' back".

"Gerrint' back" 'e 'ad said, so ah thowt a'd best try,
an gingerly went up to t'cab,
but ah thowt 'e's a bit optimistic,
as ah looked in at t'door — —- at that gap.

Me spirits wa' sinkin' but what could a' say,
that gap only looked a foot wide
an' stuck out o' t'side wa' a 'andle
but a' wouldn't tell 'im till a'd tried.

I got up on t'step —- reight determined,
did me best, a' tried this way an' that,
embarrassed in t'end I'd to tell 'im,
I 'ad to admit 'A'M TOO FAT'!!

'E gave me a look an' shoved that seat back,
a' clambered in just like a mouse.
In me mind DIET SHEETS were appearin'
an' I felt like the size of a 'OUSE.

I'll REMEMBER our trip down to Sheffield
and at night, when my bulk 'its the sack,
a nightmarish voice, it'll 'aunt me,
from afar it'll cry "GERR INT BACK"!!!

ODE TO JACK

This poem was written for an old friend on the
occasion of his 70th birthday.

When tha wa' a little lad,
tha'd run about the street,
lakin' about wi' taws an' that,
as long as it wa' leet.

Football, 'opscotch, cricket,
games wa' that much fun,
chalk marks on t'wall for t'wicket,
sometimes tha'd 'ave to run,

a crash o' glass 'ad tell thee,
that tha'd 'it somebody's winder,
"Oh no, it wa'nt me" tha'd yell,
"Onest it wa'nt mister".

In't mornin' time for school cem round,
an' wheer wa' our Jack,
fast asleep i' bed e'd be,
a snorin' on 'is back.

IT took all 'is sisters, who,
would bawl an' yell an' shout,
Come on, gerrup our Jack, they'd yell
but you wa'n't gerrin out,

jigger off, tha'd answer,
ah want to get some kip,
but the' knew if the' di'n't shift thee,
tha'd end up gerrin' t'stick.

Time went by, an' Fotteen cem,
an time ter gerra job,
so off tha went down t'road a bit
to earn an 'onest bob.

Every day tha work't away,
an' learnt most o' thi tricks,
wi' switches, bits o' wire an' such,
at Forgrove Electrics.

It wa'nt that long, or so it seemed
afore we wor at war,
an THEN tha 'ad to do thi bit,
an' Jack becem Jack Tar.

Tha sailed on t'seas for a year or two,
riskin' life an' limb,
escortin' little boats to France
an' even back agin.

Wi thi mates tha went to t'States,
an' met some reight grand folk,
they med a gre't big fuss o' thee,
'cos tha could tell a joke,

Tha told 'em tale o' t'lion,
who 'et Albert for 'is tea,
they laughed an' laughed 'til tears ran down
an' they could 'ardly see.

Tha shopped for goodies that we'd not seen
in many an' MANY a year,
then back to t'ship tha 'ad to go,
'cos tha wa' needed 'ere.

Tha sailed the wide Atlantic,
an' arrived at England's shore,
the' told thee tha wa' due some leave
an' could come 'ome once more.

Tha cem on leave wi' Tommy Green,
who wa' one o' thi mates,
an Tommy said "Come 'ome wi' me,
seein' as it's so late".

Tha'd nivver 'eard o' Shadill,
'til tha went up theer that day,
but by,   it di'n't 'alf change thi life
in many an' many a way.

Tommy said "We'll go to t'pub
an' down a pint or two,
we'll 'appen see some o' mi mates
an a few o' t'famly too.

An' sure enough tha met 'is mates,
also 'is cousin Joan,
a bonny lass so full o' fun,
wi' a wit to match thi own.

Tha cem on leave to Shadill then,
wrote letter after letter,
tha took 'er 'ome, to meet thi folks,
thi Leaves got better an' better.

Tha got to t'stage wheer tha'd like to Wed,
an' 'ad to ask 'er Dad,
'E med thi wait that flippin' long,
tha thowt that tha'd go mad.

At last tha got thi answer,
the one tha 'oped 'e'd bring
an Joanie got to wear 'er lovely
three stone diamond ring.

Cloze wa' still on coupons,
an' things i' short supply,
but Joan she saved 'em up like mad
so that she could buy...........

'Er trousseau an' a costume,
in a bonny shade o' blue,
as well as reight smart court shoes
an a navy 'andbag too.

Four bridesmaids all were picked for t'do,
wi't Groomsman an' t'Best man,
'Er Mother 'ad been an got 'er 'at,
all t'things were goin' to plan.

August cem at long, long last,
an t'end of all that waitin',
when Joan she said "I will" to thee,
before the congregation.

Everyone cem an' wished thi well,
at t'start o' married life,
an off tha went to Guernsey
to show off thi brand new Wife.

Five years went by, well nearly,
it got to fifty three,
a baby daughter cem that May
as bonny as she could be.

The years were filled wi' 'appiness
an a bit o' sadness — — — aye,
a lot o' work, an a lot o' play
as t'years went flittin' by.

A few more years an' Joanie went,
tha 'ad ter say "Goodbye",
but even though it brok thi 'eart,
tha said that tha'd get by.

Tha froze thi food an microwaved
an' slow cooked in the pot,
tha baked all sorts o' sweet stuff,
tha did the flippin' lot.

An' now tha's gettin' older,
tha's up at crack o' leet,
wi thi washin' an' thi ironin,
then foldin 'em reight neat,

So get thissen off up to t'pub
for a few more Tetley beers,
an' we all 'ope that tha goes on,
for another SEVENTY YEARS!

PLOUGH THAT FURROW

*And now I'll go back in time......to when the fields were ploughed
the hard way. Picture the scene... it's autumn, going on winter, it's
been pouring down and it looks like there's more to come, it's cold
and the wind's howling, this man and his trusty horses have been
working all day. I've called it simply — — "Plough that furrow".*

Gee-up Daisy, come on Sal,
don't go an' slow up now
I know your tired an' so am I
but we've t'rest o' t'field to plough.

Up an' down we walk all t'day,
keepin' t'furrows straight
steady on lasses, watch it theer,
we've got ter get it reight

Shiny blades slice thru' t'fresh earth,
Seagulls, Crows an' t'Plover,
follow us every yard o' t'way
for t'worms 'at blades uncover.

The'r swoopin', dippin', screamin',
noise o' flappin' wings combines,
wi' creakin' leather an' clangin' chains,
as t'wind it 'owls an' whines.

T'sky is leaden an' so is t'soil,
I'm muck reight up to t'knee,
mi boots are gettin' 'eavier,
wish mi flask wa' full o' tea.

Black branches sway against t'grey sky
already ther's a moon,
t'light is fading fast now
but a' reckon we'll finish soon.

On we've walked from dawn 'til dusk
an' at last we've got to t'end,
come on lasses, lets go 'ome
us weary way we'll wend.

Hosses fed an' watered now,
tek t'wet clothes off an' 'eight',
then it's into bed afore I drop,
it i'nt 'alf gettin' late.

Mornin' comes round all too soon
It's five be owd Big Ben,
time to milk, then 'arness up
an' start to plough again.

But today the birds are singin',
sun's risin', t'sky's turned blue,
It's grand to be a ploughman,
I reight enjoy it — —- wouldn't you?

MONDAY WASHDAY BLUES

In the 'olden days', as the children think of it, imagine this
middle aged couple waking up on a Monday morning and
the Wife facing washing day, as it used to be.

It's Monday mornin', gerrup lad,
it's time yon fire wa' goin',
ther's sticks an' coils to gerrin t 'ouse,
so whats tha think tha's doin'.

Al' nivver get t'washin' done today,
liggin theer 'til after six,
so get thi' up an gerrit lit
wi t'paper, match an' sticks.

Fires goin now, an' t'kettles boiled,
at last it's gerrin' 'ot,
but we 'aven't time to get thawed out,
we certainly 'ave not.

'E sez al' just get t'shovel,
as 'e puts down 'is pint pot,
then teks t'ot coils from t'fire
to put under t'owd Setpot.

It's all filled up wi' watter,
that's bin browt from t'pump up t'road,
then up comes t'rugs, an' t'tubs browt owt,
oh dear me, what a load.
    .

T'cover comes off t'mangle
wi' t'rollers med o' wood,
great big cogs an' t'andle
that goes round wi' such a thud.

Ther's t'peggy stick an' bars o' soap
as well as t'scrubbin' brush,
now gerrall t'watter into t'tub,
it's all a gret big rush.

Beds are stripped an' t'towels browt,
ther' all piled up on't' floor,
Jim Jeffreys, 'shirts' an' shimmies,
an' all the stuff wi wor'.

A' chuck all t'white cloze into t'tub,
grip t'peggy stick an' twist,
agitate fer all 'am worth,
it dun't 'alf 'urt yer wrist.

Now it's time ter rinse 'em,
so a' wring 'em out reight tight,
then purrem in t'clean watter
int' sink theer, on me right.

Next ah purrem in t'setpot,
to boil like 'Christmas puds'
pokin' em wit' wooden stick,
to gerrem into t'suds.

T'place is full o' steam bi' now,
A'm sweatin' like a bull
but next lots goin' into t'tub
an' now it's nearly full.

Swishin' an' swashin' from side to side,
then it's into t'sink the' go,
then onto t'whitewood table
to be scrubbed an' scrubbed an' so.....

On it goes, load after load,
for 'ours an' 'ours on end,
wi' t'washin', rinsin, scrubbin,
Dolly bluein' reight at t'end,

starch 'em, wring em, 'ang 'em out,
t'yards now full, tha' sees
lines an' LINES o' spotless cloze,
all blowin' in the breeze.

Time to brek off now a bit,
an' get summat to ' eight',
it's fry-up day on Mondays,
an' it's gerrin' very late.

Soon the dinner's ovver,
it di'n't tek that long,
pots are all weshed up agen,
an' put wheer the' belong.

So now it's back to t'kitchin,
to tidy up this mess,
ther's tub theer, now to empty
as well as all the rest.

Oilcloths back on t'table,
now 'ave gorrit scrubbed,
mangles dried an' so is t'tub,
an' t'rest 'ave all bin rubbed.

Now ther's t'flagstone floor to scrub,
it's done from end to end,
put t'donkey stone on t'doorstep,
oh will it NIVVER end.

A' must get coconut mattin' back,
a'm gerrin all aches an' pains,
ther's all that weshin' to gerrin
afore it starts an' rains.......

OH! WAIT A MINUTE, a'm wekkin up,
'ere I am i' bed
ah thowt that ah wer back i' time,
long afore I wer' wed

Me aches an' pains are theer alreight,
it's just mi owd rheumatics,
but aren't I glad that I'm 'ere now,
THANK GOD, FOR AUTOMATICS!!...

UPDATE ON T'NEWS

More doom and gloom, all the misery of Kosovo,
which spurred me to write this.
A few days later, peace was declared.

I reckon nowts gettin' much better
since a' wrote last about t'latest news
don't matter which paper yer reading
or which bloomin' programme yer choose.

It seems like "t'mad cows" been forgotten
cos now Kosovo's come to light
somewhere that we'd never 'eard of,
now ther talkin' o' goin' theer to fight.

It seems like them Serbs are a reight lot,
'ethnic cleansin' the' call it these days,
it's just like owd 'Itler wa' doin'.
'Istory don't seem to alter the'r ways.

Oustin' these folk from the'r 'ouses,
forcin' 'em out into t'street,
the'r menfolk wer' shot or just tekken
an' t'ouses wa' then set aleet.

T'poor beggars then set off for t'border,
as the'r 'ouses wa' bein' raised to t'ground,
a trickle of un'appy people,
wi' not enough food to go round.

Now NATO di'n't like what wa' 'appenin'.
We'll have to do something with these,
we'll rattle our sabres a bit to this man,
with a name like a Russian disease.

Well Clinton an' Blair they rattled an' talked
but 'e di'n't tek a blind bit o' gorm,
so they said the' would 'ave to go bomb 'im,
'e'd wish that 'e'd never been born.

So off went a sortié to sort 'im
an' bombed everything in the'r' sight,
even some that the' wa'n't even meant to.
It wa' "Just a mistake on that night".

Well t'trickle o' folk it got bigger,
as t'poor beggars they 'ad to escape
all t'shootin' an' t'killin' o' t'menfolk,
then goin' through all t'cruelty an' rape.

That trickle turned into a RIVER,
as undreds an' undreds the' trudged,
'omeless an' 'ungry an' footsore,
STILL Slobodan wouldn't be budged.

Then t'river turned into a TORRENT,
bi tractor an' trailer the' came,
on bikes an' on foot, —- even barrows,
for t'elderly, sick an' the lame.

I've got till a' can't bear to see 'em,
abject misery, an' grievin' an' pain,
me eyes the' fill up wi' all t'sadness,
then off go the planes once again.

I can't see the're mekkin' much progress,
wi' the'r bombs every neet ovver theer,
an' if the' keep missin' the'r targets,
we might get one or two ovver 'ere.

SWEET SHOP SECRETS

A true story from my village.

When I wa' little I remember these folk,
tekkin' a 'ouse wi' a shop,
'twas theer we bought spice wi' us coupons,
an' sometimes some crisps an' some pop.

The nice little woman who ran it,
'ad a son just a little bit weird,
us kids wa'n't quite 'appy about 'im,
this bloke wi' a big long black beard.

Nob'dy 'ad beards much i' THEM days,
only vagrants an' tramps an' suchlike,
so it wa' just a wee bit unusual,
to see someb'dy like 'im theer i' Wike.

It wa' WARTIME, an' folk talked about 'im,
"a conscientious objector" the' said,
which didn't mean owt to us kids like,
a mystery to us, wa' old Ted.

Lookin' back I expect 'e'd 'is reasons
an' 'is nerves can't 'ave been all that strong,
'cos LATER, 'e cem to a very bad end
but WE didn't know owt wa' wrong.

Now if ever I think o' that fam'ly
a' can't 'elp but smile to meself
the' remind me o' my maiden Auntie,
who once reached for t'Binoculars off t'shelf.

Now in my Aunties 'ouse wa' a delft rack
that wa' fixed onto 'er kitchen wall
an' as well as all t'plates, cups an' saucers,
t'Binoculars stood theer an' all.

'Er garden, it joined up wi' t'shop one,
an' from 'er kitchen window she saw — —
summat reight strange i' the'r garden,
disbelievin', she muttered, "Oh lor".

T'was then that she grabbed them Binoculars,
could it be reight, what she saw?
wa' someb'dy out theer in the'r garden,
a SIGHT she 'ad NOT seen afore.

It wa' pourin' wi' rain, Ted wa' out theer,
trottin' about round 'is lawn,
avvin' a rainwater shower,
as naked as t'day 'e wa' born.

It WA' a reight shock to 'er system
but a' think that it BRIGHTENED 'er day,
cos she LAUGHED when she told us about it,
an' t'Binoculars wa' on t'rack to stay.

TULIP TIME TRAUMA

A story told to me.

The'd been 'ankerin' to go off to t'bulbfields,
see Lincolnshire in spring wa' their dream.
Fields o' them lovely spring flowers,
they'd 'eard it wa' a sight to be seen.

Together they planned out their journey,
on t'motorbikes off the' would sped,
four of 'em on an adventure,
the' wouldn't 'alf enjoy it the' said.

Early next mornin' the' set off on t'trip,
wi' one lass on t'pillion at t'back,
muffled reight up to 'er eyebrows
an' 'er arms clung round t'waist o' 'er Jack.

'Is mate 'ad just got a new sidecar,
a shiny an' gleamin' two seater,
'Is pride an' joy wa' this purchase,
'cos nowt wa' too good for 'is Rita.

It wa' a nice day, t'roads wa' quiet
an' t'miles the' wa' soon eaten up.
In fact the' 'ad just about got theer,
when there cem' a big shout of 'Hey up'.

Too late, this bike shot out **before** em,
swervin', 'is brakes 'e rammed on
but on t'gravel it slid an' tipped ovver
an' t'bloke that 'ad caused it, went on.

Jack's mate sat theer **all** cut an' bleedin',
confused an' in shock 'e looked round,
'Is sidecar wa' all scratched an' dented,
as 'is mates sympathised —- cem a sound.

What's that? an' wheer's **Rita** 'e wondered,
she can't disappear wi'out trace,
agen cem' a cry that wa' shaky —-
ovver t'edge ther' appeared a white face.

49

The' wer' feelin' shook up an' reight sickened
but laughed when poor Rita revealed,
out o' t'sidecar she'd shot like a rocket
an' landed wi' t'cows in a field.

To mek' matters worse, this old woman,
cem' out an' she offered 'em tea,
then charged 10/6 for the pleasure,
when the' thowt it wa' goin' to be free.

The' never did get to them bulbfields,
couldn't face goin' on t'rest o' t'way,
all bleedin' an' scratched an' bedraggled
but the' laugh about it to this day.

DRUM ROLL AT SEA

Another story related to me.

A pair that we know, went away wi' their friends,
 the' fancied some sea an' some sun,
 the'd do all the things that yer do, do,
 the' **would** 'ave a reight lot o' fun.

T'decision wa' med' the'd go cruisin',
 T'sea wa' reight blue, t'waves wa' small
 ther'd be boozin' an' music an' dancin'
 lots o' food, even swimmin'an' all.

One day they wa' listenin' to t'music,
 folks wa' swayin' an' tappin' to t'beat,
 an' soon the' wa' gerrin up dancin',
 couldn't wait to gerron to the'r feet.

Round t'sides an' up t'steps sat these tourists,
 Japanese mainly it seemed,,
 watchin' all t'folk who were dancin'
 from under sun 'ats the' all beamed.

Waiters were tekkin' all t'orders,
 then wi trays filled wi' booze.... weavin' through
 all o'the folks that wer' dancin',
 trays 'eld up 'igh — — like the' do.

Well Annie an Rose, the' were watchin',
 then thowt the'd go dance straight away,
 music wa' that theer invitin',
 Rose said "Lets gerrup, what d'ya say?"

The' squeezed onto t'floor, it wa' **'eavin'**
 but the' waltzed an' the' tango'd wi' t'rest,
 a few rock an' rolls an' some twistin',
 the' really wa' doin' the'r best,

when all of a sudden it 'appened,
 this waiter walked reight across t'floor,
 goin' in an' out among' t'dancers,
 wi **two trays 'eld 'igh**, like before.

51

'E thowt 'e wa' bein' reight clever,
'til 'e caught Annies arm as she spun,
t'drinks the' went flyin' all ovver,
Annie toppled an' landed on t'drum.

As Annie struggled, the cymbals the' clanged,
an t'poor lass, all red faced she tried,
to gerrer self up off that drum kit,
she felt as if she could 'ave died.

'Er arms an' 'er legs the' wa' flailing
Tourists cameras wa' goin' non-stop
flashes from every direction ,
she thowt that she'd **never gerroff**

Rescued at last but that wa'n't all
t'Japs followed ' wi' t'cameras each day,
waitin' for t'next bit of action,
the' thowt she wa' **T'SHIPS CABARET !!..**

CHICKEN SURPRISE

An old story from my village.

Years ago, I 'eard a tale
about this poor old bloke
who lived bi 'is sen, in a cottage,
full o' dust an' muck an' smoke.

Kids the' would torment 'im,
when the' went outside to play.
'Ed shout an' swear an' chase 'em,
when the' knocked an' ran away.

Now mischief night cem' round one year
an' t'kids the' caught an 'en,
as t'owd lad sat theer dozin',
round t'fire to warm 'is sen.

'Is knees wer' fair up t'chimbley,
ashes reached to t'top o' t'pan,
as 'e sat theer in 'is ovvel——
them kids 'ad 'atched a plan.

The' giggled an' the' scuffled,
as the' climbed up t'chimbley stack
an' dropped that chicken down it
an' like light'nin' scrambled back.

There wa' squawkin' cacklin' cussin',
a reight commotion from inside
but kids wer' off down t'road that fast,
'e wouldn't see 'air nor 'ide.

'E oppened t'door an' t'en shot out,
it didn't seem no wuss',
except for t'shock it must 'ave 'ad,
t'owd lad could only cuss'.

But as 'e stood theer rantin',
arms flailin' —- all upset,
soot wa' flyin' off 'im
an' 'is face wa' black as jet.

The' said 'e looked reight funny
as 'e 'uffed an' puffed an' spat,
covered i' soot from 'ead to toe,
even piled up on 'is 'at — —.

SNAKES ALIVE?

*This poem was written the night after hearing the
tale of "The garden snake".
I thought it was so funny.*

One day a' looked out o' me winder,
a' blinked an' a' said to our lass,
"Just come ovver 'ere for a minute,
can you see a snake on that grass"?

She sez, "Oh give ovver, yer kiddin'
it's a twig that'll a' dropped of yon tree",
a' sez, " nay a' think that it's movin'
a'l 'ave to just go out an' see"

It wa' all curled up an' just laid theer,
a' went up as close as a' dared
a' thowt while it's cold it wont move much
but a' wa' just a little bit scared.

A' told t'next door neighbours an' we thowt for a bit,
"Do you think a bird dropped it last neet?"
"NAY, it would 'ave to be a reight big 'un,
'cos a' reckon it's as long as three feet"!!

SHE says"Well would ya' believe it,
o' them things a'm not very fond
but you know, it DOES mek me wonder
'cos t'fish ave been goin' out o' t'pond".

A' got a big pot wi' some 'oles in
an' bobbed it reight ovver this thing,
then a' looked up them animal people
an decided to give 'em a ring.

A' told 'er about thing in t'garden
an' what did she think a' should do
THEY wer' reight ovver in 'Uddersfield,
"WE can't come —- so 'appen that you— —-

—-could just go an' poke it an' see if it's live",
so a' said "Just 'ang on wi' this call"
so a' went to do what she requested
an it di'n't seem to MOVE much at all.

A' went back an' told 'er "I thowt it wa' dead",
so some'ow I 'ad to get rid,
if it warmed up a' THOWT it might WEKKEN
an' I di'n't want no 'Issin' Sid'.

Ah thowt that a'd put it in t'dustbin
but first a' would finish it off,
di'n't want DUSTBINMAN to get bitten,
if it roused when 'e took that lid off.

So a' went for me axe to do t'dirty deed,
a' knew a'd to do summat drastic.
Put its 'ead on a rock an' chopped it clean off
an would you believe— — — IT WA' PLASTIC !!!!!
.

AN' 'ERE IS THE NEWS - PART 3

A follow-up to my other news items.

Well now that we're into 2000
a' can't see that 'owt 'as changed much,
soon t'bit of excitement wa' ovver
an' we're back wi' all t'misery an' such.

Now t'Russians are doin' some fightin'
just like t'Kosovans did before.
Poor devil's stand theer in the'r ruins,
all ther' 'omes in a pile theer on t'floor.

At least this time WE'RE not goin' bombin',
we're mindin' us business at last,
it seems like we're keepin' us nose out,
learnin' a bit from us past.

But 'appen ther's OTHER good reasons,
which I'M 'ardly likely to know.
So we leave it to Blair an' 'is cronies.
they KNOW...... well we LIKE to think so.

Then in Africa t'weather turned savage,
it rained an' then rained an' then more,
til thousands o' miles the' wer' flooded,
folks an' animals perished by t'score.

The' clung to the roofs an' the treetops,
muddy watter it swirled down below,
one lass, she gave birth in the branches,
'ow both clung an' survived I don't know.

Everyday we saw scenes that wa' AWFUL,
an' t'rescuers they were so brave,
'Elicopters they 'ovvered o'er t'watter
an' got everyone out they could save.

One day when t'rain stopped, things looked brighter,
    then t'rain clouds cem' back at a pace,
    all t'animals bodies went floatin' away
    an' the'r crops 'ad all gone wi'out trace.

As t'watter subsided more problems began,
    after prayin' that t'rain it 'd cease,
    'cos then t'bodies polluted the watter,
    so t'next thing wa' t'fear o' disease.

We watched it an' felt for t'poor beggars
    an' then before we'd time to think,
    in Austria an avalanche 'appened,
    12 instructors 'ad died in a wink.

Next, we saw film o' Uganda,
    blokes down in mass graves, wearin' masks,
    diggin' up more an' more bodies,
    in that 'eat, wi' all t'smells, what a task.

Nine 'undred an' forty they've dug up so far,
    an' they think ther' might even be more,
    Cult members, the' now say were murdered,
    by someb'dy, more rich than before.

Fed up wi' T.V. I read t'PAPER,
    but bad news again caught mi' eye,
    4 shootin's reight 'ere in this district,
    be' fellers, in cars, goin' by.

This is ENGLAND, a' just can't believe it,
    what's 'appenin' to t'place we call 'ome,
    all t'theivin' an' muggin an' murders,
    I'm reight sure that I'm not alone —-

In feelin' reight sad at the state o' things now,
    in this country that we 'old so dear,
    bars are now fitted to t'windows,
    women go out at night full o' fear.

Folks 'ave jewell'ry dragged off the'r fingers,
the'r 'andbags are dragged off the'r arms.
Little old ladies are robbed in the'r flats,
in spite o' peep-'oles an' alarms.

Why is it 'appenin', why can't we go back,
to days when we didn't lock us doors,
our Mum's the' went out an' just left 'em,
an' nob'dy touched OWT that wa' yours.

At night yer could go for a walk on yer own,
wi'out any worries or fears,
if yer 'appened to read of a murder,
you'd all talk about it for years.

But a' reckon ther's no turnin' t'clock back,
just get on wi' yer life, wi' a smile
but it's nice to gerron to yer soapbox
an' witter just once in a while.

Meanwhile on T.V. it wa' t'Oscars again
but this year 'they'd' gone on a trip.
Folks the' wer' in a reight panic,
'til the' turned up again —- in a SKIP!

SAVED, so t'night cem', wi' all t'dazzle an' 'ype,
as t'Oscars wer' doled out again.
t'Stars wer' done up like dogs dinners
'opin' that it could be them —-

that'd stand theer an' get t'gleamin' Oscars
an' smile thru' the'r tears —- an' then tell ,
'Ow its all thanks to Mommy an' Daddy —-
an' t'Dog an' t'Canary as well.

59

EARWIGGIN

Naughty but fun, hearing snippets of other peoples'
conversations.

I love to 'ear other folk talkin',
but mi 'earin' could do wi' a test,
as I only 'ear 'ALF what ther' sayin'
an' am DYIN' to 'ear all the rest.

Ther's reight funny snippets on t'buses,
or anywhere where ther's a crowd,
a'm dyin' to 'ear t'rest o' t'sentence,
A' WISH THE' WOULD SHOUT IT OUT LOUD.

Then ther ar't folk 'at get words wrong
an' a' think we ALL do it at times',
but FUNNY when other folk do it,
so a've put one or two in mi rhymes.

T'estate agent said, said this woman,
as she travelled on t'number eight route,
yer don't get a 'ouse wi' a POPULAR,
cos t'branches go as far as it's root.

An somebody 'ad been on a 'flyer',
it sounded excitin' ter me,
It turned out she'd been playin' BINGO,
it shows just 'ow wrong yer can be.

An while we're on't subject o' bingo,
a REGULAR player we 'eard
went on a trip down to London,
an' we thowt that we MUST 'ave mis'eard,

Cos she wa'nt any real kind o' beauty,
but as this 'ear story unfurled,
we couldn't believe WHAT we wor 'earin',
'cos the' said that she'd won the MISS WORLD.

A neighbour once talked about 'speedin'',
down t'M1, to SCARBORO', she said,
a Ford ANGULAR, wa' t'vehicle i' question,
an' she really believed what she said.

An what about t'chap who wa' swimmin',
wi' ease under t'watter 'ed glide,
just like a PAPOOSE, said this woman,
as she peered in an' watched 'im from t'side.

Then a friend of ours worked in Electrics,
an while servin' in t'shop on this day,
she wa' asked fer a new DUREX 'eater,
"certainly madam" wa' all she could say,

stiflin' a grin she remembered,
'er Mother in law tellin' a friend,
of t'CONSERVATIVE somebody wa' buildin',
on t'back of the'r 'ouse,   to extend,.

Someb'dy BOASTED about 'er rice puddin',
reight creamy - not wattery an' thin,
she said what med 'er puddin special,
wa' t'EVACUATED milk she put in.

But MINE wa t'worst boob of any
A' cringe about IT to this day,
as a' sat theer at t'table wi' t'famly,
in mi teens, an' proceeded ter say,

that a friend wa'nt so well an' wer coughin',
she'd been sent to bed , for some rest,
an t'Doctor 'ad said, that she should rub 'er chest,
wi' CASTRATED OIL, ... it wa' t'best !!.......

ENGLISH AS SPOKKEN

Tired of all the 'Americanisms' and modern
lingo creeping into our language.

Summat's 'appenin' to our English language,
it's foreign an' fractured an' wrong,
why is it no longer REAL English,
American talk don't belong.

We're no longer workin' to schedule,
we do it to SKEDULE, you see,
'cos we've GOTTEN this new sort o' lingo
an' even more IMPORTANTLEE — —

GRASS ROOTS LEVEL is where we get back to,
at this MOMENT IN TIME —- so they say,
BASICALLY it's just this new language,
new expressions to learn everyday.

There's, "CAN YOUI JUST RUN THAT ONE PAST ME"
through 'em is more 'ow yer feel,
then SUDDENLY everythings "PEAR SHAPED"
an' I must take a "RAIN CHECK" they squeal.

Bewildered, this feller 'as now "LOST THE PLOT"
so tries for a date with a "SHRINK",
who looks for a "WINDOW" in't diary
an' then "WE'LL TOUCH BASE" what d'ya think?

Ideas are "BOUNCED OFF YER" in these days
an' "RUN THIS ONE PAST ME" the' say,
then ask yer for some "BALL PARK FIGURES"
wi' LEARNIN' CURVES'mentioned each day,

Our Students now gather on 'CAMPUS',
tek 'VACATIONS' instead of a break,
in the'r free time the' go to a 'MOVIE',
an' a 'SABBATICAL's' summat they take.

Can't the' just tek a 'oliday, like we do,
why don't the' use English like me?
bring BACK all t'real English as spokken,
by Yorkshire folk — — — especialeee!! .

MAN TALK

Maybe the least said about this the better.

Where's me keys 'e shouted?
after rummagin' in t'drawer.
Ah put em in theer yesterd'y,
she says, "They 'aven't gone far".

Well **I** can't understand it,
you should leave **MY** things alone
I know **EXACTLY** wheer I put em.
in t'drawer theer, reight bi t'phone.

She says, "'ave yer tried yer pockets?".
'E replied "the' wer in that drawer,
yer must 'ave gone an' moved 'em,
o' that I'm bloomin' sure.

Off she crossed to t'sideboard
an' oppened up that drawer,
she parted things at t'top of it
an' what do yer think she saw.

A bunch o' keys lay shinin' theer,
an **inch** from t'usual place.
Suspiciously 'e looked at 'er,
'e 'ad to save 'is face.

'E muttered a bit an then swore blind,
that t'keys wa'n't theer **before**.
Felt sure she'd somehow sneaked 'em in,
when 'e'd turned to go through t'door.

next its.....
"ave yer seen t'screwdriver?"
She sez "What do yer think?
a' just knocked up a shelf or two
when I'd finished pots in t'sink"!!.

'E sez, "Well **somebody's** 'ad it,
it **should** be theer in t'box".
Sarcastically she glared at 'im,
"Aye, I wa' goin' to change all t'locks".

Later on, it's peace at last
an' she 'ad a peep through t'door,
theer 'e wa' wi a bit o' wood
an' t'screwdriver on t'floor.

She sez "I see you've found it".
T'answer cem through gritted teeth.
"Well **I** di'n't purrit away like **that**,
it 'ad got reight underneath". .

64

WHO NEEDS ENEMIES?

*This next one I wrote after getting really fed up with
my neighbour who came and whined at me several
times a week and ALWAYS came to keep me company
whilst I was ironing on a Monday. She was completely
tactless and had no idea that she was. I've called it:-
Who needs enemies?*

It's lookin' a bit dark an' dismal,
don't look very promisin' to me,
so I think I'll not bother wi' t'washin',
I'll just go see Pat for some tea.

I don't think she'll be ALL that busy,
a dustin' an' vaccin' an' that,
so I think I'll just pop round an' see 'er,
I could do wi' a nice little chat.

I can tell 'er the tale o' mi bunions
an' 'ow they are painin' me, chronic,
'ow me nerves mek me feel 'ungry,
'spect she'll say I could do wi' a tonic.

I could ask 'er advice on mi 'air an' mi feet,
an where I can get 'em done right,
but p'raps it's as well to go where I know,
I might end up lookin' a sight.

I tell 'er mi cloze all seem frumpy an' old,
an' I seem to 'ave lost all mi style,
but SHE always seems to drop lucky,
wish I could get things from a pile.

She got all them things from 'er sister,
who died earlier on in the year,
I tell 'er "My word you are LUCKY"
she does seem to look at me queer!.

I can tell 'er again, 'ow much better t'place looks,
now that ther' gettin' things done,
she'll be reight pleased to know that a've noticed
cos the' didn't 'ave much when the' come.

Mi 'usband 'e fusses about 'er,
when she buys stuff in t'shop for ther' tea
but I send 'im out to get t'taties
cos 'e don't talk like that much to me.

'E tells 'er she's looking; reight bonny,
an brightens reight up when she's there,
I tell 'er she's lost all 'er glamour
now she's not bleachin' 'er 'air.

I reckon bi now she'll be ironin'
so I'll go round an' get t'cuppa tea,
it's NICE to 'ave some'dy to chat to,
She's just like a DAUGHTER to me.

SLIMMING CLUB BLUES

I'm sure this poem will sound very familiar to anyone
who has ever felt the need of a 'SLIMMING CLUB'.

I walk down t'club an' am quakin',
cos a' know that a'v' put on some weight,
will she let it be known to the rest o' the class,
p'raps a' might just turn up late.

An' then if a' tek off me cardi'
an' rush out an' 'ave one more wee,
a' could be a little bit lighter
 so she won't tek much notice o' me

Yes, a'v been very good, stuck to t'diet
so I don't know WHY a'v not lost,
Yes, it was just one SMALL bar o' chocolate,
a' slipped up a' know, to me cost.

A' come from a very fat famly,
an' you'll notice a'm very big boned,
so a' can't see a'l EVER be skinny,
a'l p'raps go to t'gym an' get TONED.

A'v follered t'instructions to t'letter
I 'ardly eat owt, ask our Dorrie,
Oh! ther' wa' that theer belly pork sandwich
I et while a' sat watchin' Corrie!

A'v' read that theer book, til a'm cross eed,
 wi' carbohydrates an' proteins a'v tussled,
a'm not all that fat do you reckon?
,a lot of it could just be muscle.

FOTTEEN STONE, do you say, nay t'scales must be wrong
a'v nivver weighed THAT i' me life,
a' just can't believe it, so what can I do?
its causin' me no end o' strife.

CUT DOWN on me fryin' an' sugar,
me CREAM CAKES an' BISCUITS as well,
them big YORKSHIRE PUDS on a Sundy,
it sounds like its goin' to be 'ell.

Oh blow it, a'v got some nice French bread,
an' a'v made some nice raspberry jam
a' can't give up EVERY enjoyment,
So dammit, a'll stop as I am.

WHO NEEDS HOLIDAYS?

Written after a disastrous holiday in Majorca.

T'four on us went for a brek an' a rest,
a reight one it turned out to be.
We'd all of us luggage to carry up t'ill,
an' t'otel it wa' nowhere near t'sea

We staggered up t'ill an' wa' jiggered
an' us spirits the' sank to us feet
when receptionist said' when we asked about food
"I'm sorry your too late to eat"!

We'd to stagger back down an' realized our plight,
stoppin' at t'top o' that 'ill,
we'd never be able to go anywhere,
wi'out gaspin' for breath an' a pill.

We just CAN'T stop 'ere, we MUST see a Rep,
an' its AWFUL' we're stuck in a town,
we can't see we'll ever get down t'steps to t'sea,
or get BACK, if we ever get down.

At last we saw t'Rep, who said 'e couldn't 'elp,
the' really wa' nowt 'e could do,
we SHOULDN'T a' booked on a late break
wi' 'eart trouble an' other things too!

Well t'next day, it WASN'T a good day,
we should 'ave all just stopped i' bed,
Roy picked up a chair bi' the poolside
an' a tree branch, it stuck in 'is 'ead.

69

They'd lopped this 'ere Lemon tree down bi' the pool,
leaves 'ad grown so t'sharp bit wa' obscured,
a' looked round when Roy asked for a tissue,
as from under 'is 'and, the blood poured.

It turned out to be not as bad as it looked
an' t'manager 'e cleaned up Roy's 'ead,
then said "e could 'ave a free Cognac,
to mek' 'im feel better", 'e said.

Later we thowt we'd risk walkin' down t'road,
t'adventure 'ad 'ardly begun,
when Jean's feet the' went skiddin' ont' footpath,
an' groanin' she sat on 'er bum!

She'd twisted 'er leg underneath 'er,
fell down wi' a scream an' a shout.
"It's me leg, it's me leg, I'm in agony"
an' wi' that she wa' goin' to pass out.

Roy managed to get 'er a taxi
an' back to t'otel we all went,
where the' then 'ad to send for a doctor,
who glanced at 'er leg - an' then went.

8,000 pesetas 'e charged 'er
an' t'Ambulance soon it appeared,
so Roy an' me thowt we'd go shoppin'
but 'is wallet 'ad then disappeared.

We rushed back in t'lounge, where we'd waited wi' Jean,
an' we searched an' we searched 'igh an' low,
we lifted all t'cushions an shifted all t'chairs,
it wa'nt theer, so where else could we go,

THEN, Roy remembered 'ow 'ed been in t'loo,
where 'ed wetted 'is 'anky for Jean,
to ease t'pain in 'er leg, THEN 'e found it,
on't floor tiles, it could 'ardly be seen.

Hooray! luck at last, Roy went back to t'shop,
an at last all our shoppin' wa' got
but then Jean an' Alan cem back in a cab
an she 'ad 'er leg in a POT.

Gleamin an' white an' reight up to 'er knee,
wi' two crutches, she struggled int' door
an' THEN they announced that THEY wer' off 'ome,
the' REALLY couldn't cope theer no more.

We wa' tekken' aback, but we DID understand,
that NOW the' couldn't go out at ALL,
the'd be stuck int' 'otel or bi't pool everyday,
if ONLY she 'adn't 'ad that fall.

After lots o' discussin' an' talks wi' First Choice,
we wer' offered apartments instead,
if not, we'd to pay fifty four pounds more each
an' we couldn't afford THAT much, we said.

Rob an' Lyn, a nice couple we'd met ont' first day,
did ALL that the' could do to 'elp,
Rob even 'elped carry Jean up an' downstairs,
the' both wer' just kindness itself.

Jean couldn't cope wi' 'er crutches,
'ad a reight funny turn in a lift,
so Rob, 'e demanded a wheelchair,
at reception, they looked a bit miffed.

71

But t'chair, it wa' duly delivered
as she sat bi the pool on that day,
an' we'd gone to suss out t'apartments,
then got a bus back theer to say,

They'd let us look round an' it din't look 'alf bad
an' t'sea, it wa'n't that far away,
we could even get to it wi' t'wheelchair,
at LAST, we've found somewhere to stay.

We couldn't move in theer til't Sat'd'y,
so we made t'best of t'hotel 'til then,
Rob an' Lyn, they 'elped push that old wheelchair,
back up an' down' t'ill, once again.

Well t'Sat'd'y came round an' Jean went off that day,
to t'clinic to get a new pot.
Then in taxis we went to t'apartments.
tekkin t'wheelchair an' t'baggage an' t'lot.

Well, we di'n't get us rooms that the'd promised
we'd to wait, then wer' given a key,
up ont' first floor they 'ad put us,
so we all made to go up an' see.

Well t'gremlins, they must 'ave gone with us,
'cos then t'LIFT wouldn't work, just refused,
so wi' that Rob an' Lyn carried bags up them stairs
an' ont' corridor we traipsed — not amused.

We staggered wi't baggage an' found t'other lift
an' EVENTUALLY we got it to work,
UMPTEEN TIMES, we'd to press that theer button,
then it went wi' a bump an' a jerk.

Jean an' Alan, they wer'nt quite so lucky,
as t'lift went an' stopped far too soon,
so they 'ad a reight job gettin' t'chair ovver t'step
an' in tears, Jean arrived at the room.

At t'opposite end Roy an' me found our room,
we 'eard 'ammering an' bangin' an' that,
t'Joiners 'ad our bed settee upside down
an' t'maids wa' still workin' in't flat.

Will it all nivver end, this 'ere nightmare,
will our 'oliday one day begin,
can we all settle down an' enjoy it
an' our room, will we EVER get in?

We all 'ad a meal an a look at the sea,
then fancied an earlier night
but found t'Karaoke wa' startin,
reight under our room — at t'poolside.

T'stage, it wa' reight underneath us,
music pounded an' boomed, voices sang,
we at last fell asleep, fair exhausted,
then wa' wekkend at six — wi' a bang.

It's TORTURE, us nerves they wa' janglin'
as we 'eard all that noise from next door,
bangin' all't drawers an' ther' cubbards,
then draggin' ther' cases crosst' floor.

Next day the' did move us an' things they improved
but then when Roy took off 'is specs,
'Is eye it wa' pulsin' an' black as could be
I despaired an' thowt "oh 'eck, what next"?

Wa' this owt to do wi' that cut on 'is 'ead,
I prayed that 'e would be alright,
what wi' Jean i' plaster an' cuts an' black eyes,
'Ope t'end of all this lots i' sight.

Jean an' Alan kept tryin' to talk wi' a Rep,
some'ow one could NEVER be seen,
Roy went down wi' 'em to try once again,
'e'd gone —- but they said that 'e'd been.

That night we went out an' found somewheer to eat,
a place run by a bright Cockney bloke.
'E soon med a space for Jean's wheelchair
an' wa' laughin' an' jokin' wi' folk.

It reight cheered us up, we enjoyed it,
then back for a brandy in't' room,
outside they wa' 'aving a quiz night,
then t'music, it started to boom.

T'quiz night an' t'music went on 'alf o't'night
but Alan, who's nobody's fool,
wa' up bright an' early wi't' towels,
to put 'em on't' chairs beside t'pool.

Alan phoned Rob an' Lyn on that Monday
an' they told 'im they'd 'ired a car,
so after a bit the' cem ovver
an' we all sat bi't pool an' the bar.

Roy an' Alan went in an they made a nice meal,
then we all went to see Magalluf,
Rob an' Lyn even went parascendin',
reight brave, doin' that sort o' stuff.

Jean an' Alan 'ad planned on US 'iring a car
an' we really did want to see't' place
but it got more embarrassin' bi't minute,
as OUR funds began to sink wi'out trace.

We'd paid for 'alf board at t'hotel theer,
just took money for snacks an' to spend,
didn,t bargain for 'avin' to buy all us food,
our cash wouldn't last us 'til t'end.

Then Alan cem up wi' the answer,
said it wa' THEIR fault we 'ad to move on.
'E said they'd provide all the dinners
to buy or to cook from then on.

We DID get a car an the six of us went
an' we DID see some really grand sights,
climbin' mountains to Soller, Alcudias walls,
Porto Cristo an Formentor's 'ights.

The beaches wa' sandy an' t'sea it wa' warm,
when we went in to 'ave a quick dip,
sun it beat down from a sky blue as blue
we really did 'ave a good trip.

While we wa' out on that couple o' days,
Jean an' Alan wa' wanted on't' phone,
t'Insurance firm wanted to tell 'em,
about 'ow they 'ad to get 'ome.

Jean's leg 'ad to be kept up on't' journey,
she needed THREE seats, t'clinic said
but t'seats wa' all booked up to Yeadon,
they'd to go via Gatwick i'stead,

The' then 'ad to travel bi' taxi
an' leave t'wheelchair an' crutches be'ind,
Alan didn't know 'OW the' would manage,
'e wa' nearly goin' out of 'is mind.

Next few days the' went by wi'out trouble,
from Majorca we then took us leave,
Roy an' me, we then flew back to Yeadon,
leavin' Alan wi' 'is luggage — an Jean

'E managed but t'nightmare wa'n't over,
they got theer to Gatwick alright,
then they couldn't get up to get t'taxi,
it looked like they'd be theer all night.

T'lift wouldn't work, they wa' sent in a room
along wi' five other folk too,
they wa' stuck theer for nearly two 'ours
so they didn't get 'ome until two.

Now t'oliday nightmare is over
and t'end of all t'trauma an' worry,
it's grand to be back 'ome in England
but we won't forget THAT in a 'urry.

COMPULSIVE VIEWIN'

What is the attraction of accidents? Living then beside
a busy main road where they happened quite often, we
got used to the sound of sirens and people suddenly
appearing — — usually with dogs!!.

There goes t'sirens, off again,
it's like livin' in New York.
Erm! I'll just tek t'dog up t'road a bit
a' think 'e needs a walk.

"Ow do Bill" grand day again,
but a' think ther's summat up
thowt I'd stretch me legs a bit
an' exercise our pup.

Aye, 'our Bob' could do a walk,
I'll just go get is chain
an' walk down t'road wi thee a bit
a' wa' goin' to go up t'lane.

Ee, look down theer, a' think they've stopped,
ther's another flashin' leet ,
we could mebbe go down t'road a bit,
instead of up yon street.

Ther's t'Amb'lance now an' t'Police as well
a' reckon its been a bad 'un,
now ther's t'Fire brigade an' all
aye! some'dys day's a sad 'un.

Traffic's all stopped an' buildin' up,
Bill an' Tom they stop an' talk,
gates keep oppenin' an' folk come out,
they ALL seem to need a walk.

Bill sez, "av' nivver seen 'IM before,
e's genrally in 'is car,
an THAT one nivver walks ANYWHEER
'E only props up t'bar.

Kids come runnin' down to see
What t'noise is all about
on skateboards an the'r mountainbikes
the' don't want to miss out.

By t' time all troubles sorted
ther's a reight crowd 'ovverin' theer
just on t'sidelines so to speak
reight COURAGEOUS wi' no fear

Funny thing is, they most 'ave DOGS,
bein' dragged from out the'r drives
I'm SURE they've nivver been walks before,
nivver in all the'r lives.

Ah swear some of 'em borrow 'em
for occasions such as THIS
It'll be "Can I take your Rover out"?
or all t'accidents the'd miss.

Funny, this FASCINATION
wi' 'orror, blood an' gore,
yet if the' needed an INJECTION,
the'd be scared to go through t'door.

WHO NEEDS SKY?
(when you can have a digi-box)

This story is absolutely true.
The lengths we had to go to, to get the Digibox
plus all the accompanying problems.

We could do wi one o' them boxes!
puzzled an' lookin' nonplussed,
She answered, " Well what sort o' boxes?".
E' says, "Oh, the' say ther' a must".

Them 'things' to put on yer telly,
so folks can get programmes galore.
She sez, "Well, ther's only ONE, WE watch,
so I don't know what WE want one for".

Well you'll 'ave a reight choice o' viewin',
wi' Sky news goin' on all day long,
ther'll be sport an' channels for shoppin',
reight bargains, stuff goin' for a song.

If YOU miss yer 'soaps' yer can see 'em on theer,
'e'd nearly convinced 'er be then,
but she 'oped that it wouldn't be costly.
'e says "Don't WORRY thissen".

'E went bargain 'untin' next mornin',
The' told 'im, yer just plug it in!
but of course things are never THAT simple
wi' no scart plug to plug the thing in!!

Telly wa' old, an' wi'out one,
so 'e tussled wi' plugs, wires as well
tryin' to get em a picture,
all the while ther' wa' this funny smell.

'E phoned up the makers next mornin'
who agreed that ther' wa' summat wrong
The' said tek it back where yer got it
ther' shouldn't be a warm burnin' pong!!

79

Well THAT shop 'ad sold out o' the bargains,
to another branch the' 'ad to go,
but thing wa' exchanged wi' no problem.
Do you think things wa' sorted — — —OH NO!!

'E opened up t'box an' t'remote wa'n't theer
an' some'ow this smell, it still lurked.
'E began to think it might be t'telly,
it wa' gettin' OLD, but it WORKED

Next day back the' went to swop that theer box.
No problem at all wi' the Firm,
after that the' went lookin' for Telly's
in case THEIRS wa' ready to burn.

She'd made 'im unplug it at bedtime
this strange smell wa' really no joke,
frightened that if the' just left it,
apartments might go up in smoke.

Off 'ome the' went wi' t'new Telly
complete wi' a scart plug as well.
Then 'e took out t'new box from it's packin'
an' lookin' in theer 'is face fell,

'Cos this time t'TRANSFORMER wa' missin',
like old Victor Meldrew 'e yelled,
"I really don't want to believe it"
an' still ther' wa that funny smell!!

First thing next day off the' went once again,
sayin' this time "Enough is enough",
So t'money refunded, the' shopped somewhere else
an cem 'ome wi' a box made by BUSH

Success at last, 'e got the thing fixed
'E whizzed round t'new channels wi' glee
but STILL this strange odour wa' lurkin'
it's a NIGHTMARE just what can it be?

Early next day the smell wa' still theer,
they'd felt an' they'd sniffed every plug
an' what do you think wa' the culprit?
some LILIES stuck theer in a jug!!!

SUPERMARKET FUN

The joys of shopping, coming up to a bank holiday.
Instead of Morrisons, you could be in ASDA, Tesco,
Sainsburys, etcetera.

Come on, let's go to Morrisons,
we'll do a reight good shop.
Ther's goin ter be a 'oliday,
let's fill t'trolley up to t'top.

First ther's parkin' problem,
all t'disabled spaces gone,
so round an' round the park you go,
for goodness knows 'ow long.

At last yer yell "Oh theers a space,
lets just get in, reight sharp",
but bi t'time you've done manoeuvrin'
someb'dy's beat yer — — what a lark.

Ther's summat really funny,
when a 'oliday is due,
you'd think shop wa' shut a fortnight,
believe ME —- I'm tellin' you.

They overflow them trolleys,
wi' every kind of stuff
the'r really on a mission,
MUST be SURE they've got enough.

They rush round t'aisles in a frenzy,
an offer — — oh look —- two for one
an' then 50p off that other
an' we've ONLY just BEGUN.

She wonders about buyin' mushrooms,
'e says, "Oh they'll only go off".
she says,"Well I could always use 'em
for BREAKFAST or in t'Stroganoff".

What about tomatoes then,
ther's some nice ones theer on t'vine.
'e says "Will you use 'em?"
"I'm sure I will — — i' time".

'E says, "ther's nobody comin'
ther'll only be you an' me,
we don't NEED all this flippin' stuff".
she mutters "Oh! we'll see ".

'E says,"I wish these trolley wheels
would go in a straight line
it WOULD make life easier
an' save a lot o' time"

Two for one an' three for two,
we wont 'ave much to spend.,
watch Kamikazi pensioners
stormin' round that bend.

Fruit an' veg an t'salad bar
an' we'd better 'ave some 'am,
oh 'eck! We need a ticket,
so to t'end o' t'queue the' ran.

Ther's folk theer reight determined,
buyin' loads o' this an' that.
'Am an' Tongue an Beef an' Pork,
"I want it LEAN —- NO FAT!"

Next pork pies an' sausage rolls,
pickles, crisps, of every sort'
I wish they'd shut that kiddy up,
I'm gettin' overwrought.

It's now screamin' blue murder,
as its Mum fills t'cart to t'brim,
too busy wi' this shoppin',
to care what's botherin' 'im.

Bread an' cakes an' biscuits
an' goodies by the score.
oh dash! that wheel is off again,
we'll knock someone for sure.

Packets o' this an' packets o' that,
Yoghourts, milk an' marg,
as well as all the party stuff.
OUR bill will be reight large.

'E says "Lets pack it in now,
lets go an' 'ave a cuppa'
I can see us still doin' t'shoppin'
when it's time to 'ave us supper".

To t'checkout off the' toddle,
this whoppin' bill to pay,
layin' siege —- oh what a farce,
T'SHOPS ONLY CLOSED ONE DAY!!

SPC

AND HERE IS THE NEWS 05

It's a long time since I last did a news bit,
  so ah reckon ther' must be one due
tho' ah can't see ther's been many changes
  folks are still carryin' on, like the' do.

Worst thing seems to me, t'war in Iraq,
yes, they went in AGAIN — —- so whats new?
tho' this time old Tony, instigated bi' Bush,
  would go on to t'end — —- see it through.

Right, so they made it, all t'way to Baghdad
  Saddam's effigy came a tumblin',
what they achieved, it's still hard to know
  wi' most of t'Iraqui's still grumblin'.

It didn't turn out as expected,
  Iraqui's thowt they would be free,
  free o' Saddam an' 'is cruelty
but seems like things wa'n't meant to be.

Instead ther' wa' lootin' an' killin'
  an' t'Yanks mekkin' t'usual blunders,
killin' ours, ther' own and t'Iraqui's.
  You despair an' CAN only wonder!!

What did t'war start for int' first place,
  Blair insisted they'd weapons SO bad
so called 'weapons of mass destruction',
  could wipe us all out, could old 'Sad'.

But when the' got theer an' went searchin'.
  not a solitary thing cem' to light
  but Tony 'e kept on insistin'
that the' wer' 'idden theer, 'e wa' right.

Well a few years'ave passed since the skirmish
  yet a lot of our Troops are still there
no doubt wishin' that they wa' in England
  an' not thinkin' too kindly o' Blair.

But NOW all the news it 'as altered
now Iraq it gets 'ARDLY a mention
cos' 'ere we are in 2005
an' 'eadin' for t'general election.

On t'telly reporters are chasin' about
length an' t'breadth o' the country the' reach
followin' all t'Politicians,
'angin' on to each word — —- every speech.

'Ow do you choose who to vote for?
when life it will be SO MUCH BETTER,
with WHOEVER gets in,
they've spelled it all out — — to the letter.

All t'Ospitals will gleam wi' the polish,
no germ will dare enter that door,
Jeyes fluid will permeate t'buildin',
wi' a Matron in charge o' each floor.

Patients'll arrive for appointments,
Nurses'll be everywhere,
no need to worry about waitin'
ther'll be that many Doctors in there.

If your complaint 'appens to be serious,
no worries about findin' a bed,
you'll find yourself in it, in barely a 'minute',
your 'op' done at t'nod of a 'ead.

Students will no longer pay owt,
they'll cease to be thousands in debt.
Wi' this 'Life o' Riley', they'll all become 'Smiley'
instead of all t'worry the' get.

We'll 'ave Teachers galore, so t'classes are small
An' we'll see tons o' Bobby's on't beat,
we'll see good behaviour an' streets'll be safer,
so us 'Oldies' dare go out at neet,.

Also for us 'Oldies' life will be great,
we'll 'ardly be payin' owt at all,
wi' free this an' that an' no taxes,
I guess we'll be 'avin' a ball.

We'll be jettin' all ovver — — won't see us for dust
an' not just to Spain anymore,
It'll be long haul flights, an' in Club Class,
Yippee!!...... but 'ang on , are we sure?

Does it all sound too perfect I wonder,
as these promises an' stories the' weave,
are WE a lot clearer now WE know the facts?
I still don't know WHO to believe.